T0329289

ST JOHN OF THE CROSS

ST JOHN *of* THE CROSS

by

E. ALLISON PEERS

Sometime Scholar of Christ's College
Professor of Spanish in the
University of Liverpool

THE REDE LECTURE FOR 1932

CAMBRIDGE

AT THE UNIVERSITY PRESS

1932

CAMBRIDGE
UNIVERSITY PRESS

University Printing House, Cambridge CB2 8BS, United Kingdom

Published in the United States of America by Cambridge University Press, New York

Cambridge University Press is part of the University of Cambridge.

It furthers the University's mission by disseminating knowledge in the pursuit of
education, learning and research at the highest international levels of excellence.

www.cambridge.org
Information on this title: www.cambridge.org/9781107651326

© Cambridge University Press 1932

First published 1932
Re-issued 2014

A catalogue record for this publication is available from the British Library

ISBN 978-1-107-65132-6 Paperback

Cambridge University Press has no responsibility for the persistence or accuracy of
URLs for external or third-party internet websites referred to in this publication,
and does not guarantee that any content on such websites is, or will remain, accurate
or appropriate.

PREFATORY NOTE

This treatment of the life and work of St John of the Cross in relation to the world of to-day, having to be brought within the limits of a single lecture, is necessarily brief and suggestive rather than in any one of its divisions complete. I have tried, by means of footnote references, to avoid repeating at length anything that has already been said in the chapter on St John of the Cross in my *Studies of the Spanish Mystics*. A few other indications are given, both bibliographical and critical, which may profitably be followed up by readers interested in the subject.

The text of the lecture is printed exactly as it was delivered.

E. A. P.

6 *May* 1932

ST JOHN OF THE CROSS

There is always a deep and rare satisfaction in the study of a single man, or of a single work of art, that is of true eminence. Many a young scholar has entered upon research in some remote corner of the field of the humanities, and, after a brief experience, has turned from it in impatience at the deadening effect of the constant study of second-rate and third-rate minds. In many literatures there have been whole eras, which, for historical reasons, have of necessity to be studied, yet in which is found the name of no single author of real distinction, and in which, amid numerous works of immense and forbidding magnitude, there occurs none that can lay claim to greatness. Happy the moment which in any nation sees the birth of some new and outstanding genius, or at which a new light plays upon some surpassingly great genius of the past and guides men to a fresh study of his achievements. For there is that in the work of such a man which, at each new contact, both refreshes and enkindles the imagination. It matters not if his eminence seek expression in some resounding material triumph, in the world of ideas or in the domain of pure spirit. "Flame is flame wherever you find it." And the flame of genius "blazes with new glories" whenever and wherever it is rekindled.

Spain, a country indelibly stamped with individualism, has in her long and splendid past been immensely rich in men and women of this calibre. Her greatest achievements have been wrought by the intense effort of individuals rather than by the quiet and persistent co-operation and effective organization of masses. Such individuals are the semi-legendary Pelayo, Fernán González and the Cid; the mediaeval monarchs James the Conqueror and Alfonso the Wise; the discoverer Columbus (whom we may now venture to claim wholly for Spain) and the *conquistadores* who followed him; the prince of dramatic wits, Lope de

Vega, the divine and humane Cervantes, the brilliant and romantic Calderón; the painters Velázquez, Murillo, Goya; and the great company of religious reformers—St Dominic, St Vincent Ferrer, St Ignatius Loyola, St Francis Javier, St Teresa, St John of the Cross.

I have chosen to speak in this lecture of St John of the Cross—in three fields pre-eminent, as a poet, as an ascetic and as a mystic—because, after being neglected[1] or misunderstood by all save a few, he is now, somewhat rapidly, coming into his inheritance of fame. Of recent years, indeed, with the widespread revival of interest in the life of contemplation, he has been achieving something more remarkable even than fame—something akin to posthumous popularity. In Spain, the three-

---

[1] Rousselot (*Les Mystiques Espagnols*, Paris, 1867), for decades the only authority on Spanish mysticism easily available, gives St John of the Cross less than half as much space as St Teresa, less than one-third as much as Luis de León, about the same allowance as Venegas and Malón de Chaide, slightly more than Juan de Ávila and considerably less than Luis de Granada. Yet, as a mystic alone, he is immeasurably superior to any of these save St Teresa.

volume Toledo edition of his works (1912–14) —itself a great advance on its predecessors— has been completely outclassed by the five-volume edition published in Burgos (1929–31) by the learned Carmelite, P. Silverio de Santa Teresa. The relatively short space of fifteen years which separates those two editions has also seen the publication of two less important editions of the complete works and two of the commentary on the "Spiritual Canticle". During the same period there has been a flood of *sanjuanista* literature—numerous books and innumerable articles—and, though some of these are ephemeral, called forth by Pius XI's proclamation of the Saint as a Doctor of the Church Universal (August 24, 1926) and by the second centenary of his canonization (December 26, 1926), many more of them are evidence of independent interest.[1]

The abundant testimony to this interest

[1] For a select bibliography, cf. *Studies of the Spanish Mystics* (London, 1927, 1930: abbreviated hereafter *S.S.M.*), Vol. I, Nos. 554–652, Vol. II, Nos. 953–69. A third volume, with supplementary bibliography, is in preparation.

which comes from Spain is no less strikingly reinforced from abroad. In France, where translations of the complete works have long abounded, no less than four new versions of the "Spiritual Canticle" have appeared in fifteen years,[1] together with two of the most important biographies of the Saint which have ever been written. That of M. Baruzi is only the first part of a long critical study (*Saint Jean de la Croix et le problème de l'expérience mystique*, Paris, 1924) which approaches its subject from a fresh and an entirely independent standpoint. No less commendable, for quite different reasons, is a more orthodox biography, written by a Discalced Carmelite, P. Bruno de Jésus-Marie (*Saint Jean de la Croix*, Paris, 1929). This latter has been translated into English (London, 1932). In our own country, though the recent important textual reconstructions accomplished by Spanish editors now call for a new complete translation of the works, we have on the whole been well served for over

[1] That of Dom Chevallier (*Le Cantique Spirituel de Saint Jean de la Croix*, Paris, 1930) is the most remarkable.

sixty years by the felicitous, if frequently inaccurate, translations of David Lewis. Lovers of poetry have long been familiar with the versions of two of St John of the Cross's poems made by Mr Arthur Symons, which, like Lewis's translations of the prose works, are usually very true to the spirit of their original though occasionally failing as to the letter.

A general interest in what is loosely called mystical literature has been steadily growing for the last twenty years, and this by no means only in our own country. The contributions of Spain to this literature are enormous, and their importance has come to be fairly generally realized outside the Peninsula. At first, attention was focussed on the two great Carmelite Saints—*la Santa*, as the Spanish Carmelites say, and *el Santo*: I mean St Teresa and St John of the Cross. Soon, however, they came to be looked upon, no longer as the only two mystics of Spain, but rather as her two most significant figures towering above a host of others, which is their true position. But I am not at this time concerned so much with the rehabilitation of the lesser Spanish mystics as with the somewhat earlier emergence of St John of the Cross to take his rightful place beside St Teresa.[1] The frank and readable autobiography of St Teresa and her delightfully human letters have caused her to be considered, especially outside Spain, as a sort of phenomenon among the Saints, in that she lived in the closest touch with everyday life; and until recent times there has been a tendency to contrast St John of the Cross with her as a prodigy of asceticism who lived in another world of his own and wrote not so much mystical as misty treatises which the ordinary mortal can be expected neither to understand nor even to read. You would not wish me to enumerate the reasons for this conception nor to trace in detail its growth and decline: that it did exist and that it is now declining there can be no kind of doubt. As the world comes

[1] In Spain, he has always held this place: I am thinking rather of our own country, where Lewis's translations (1864 ff.) first gave it to him, and of continental countries other than Spain, where Rousselot's cavalier treatment of him for some time set the fashion.

better to understand the Saint who was so dear to Teresa of Jesus and who was no less human than she, it should decline still further. It is to be hoped that when, in ten years' time, we celebrate the quatercentenary of his birth (1542), he may have come into his own, in this country at least, as one of the most attractive, invigorating and inspiring religious writers who have ever lived.

My aim in this lecture is not to present St John of the Cross purely and simply as an historical figure, but to interpret him in terms of the twentieth century—to show him as he may well be regarded by the world of to-day —by that section of the world, that is to say, to which men of his type are naturally sympathetic. And, in order that in the brief compass of an hour-glass we may obtain as complete a view of him as possible, I propose to speak, in turn, of his life and personality, of his poetry, of his asceticism and of his mystical teaching.

I

Juan de Yepes, afterwards St John of the Cross, belonged by birth, education and predilection to Spain's austere plateau—Castile, "tierra de cantos y santos": land of boulders and of saints. Land, where the piercing winds of a long and cruel winter, the drought of a short, burning summer, the consequent barrenness of the unwatered soil and the necessary poverty of those who endeavour to drag a living from it combine to produce all the heroic virtues of sanctity—patience, perseverance, meekness, resignation, fortitude. One glorious quality, however, belongs to the Castilian table-land: "the glory of the sun—triumphant in an azure sky".[1] From its cold, clear rising to its brilliant, luminous setting it bathes the entire country in a light incredibly keen—a light that, with relentless refulgence, reveals the gently undulating, scrub-covered

[1]   Y la gloria del sol es un triunfo
en un cielo de azur.
                              (Enrique de Mesa.)

or snow-clad steppe, the pinewoods and oak-woods, the tiny, brown, distant villages, and the blue hills of the horizon.

Something of that light, it would seem, has penetrated to the archives which contain this Castilian Saint's life-story. It floods the pages of his biography, illumines all that there is of truth in scores of contemporary documents, and allows us to gaze, not merely upon the paragon of hagiographers, but upon a simple and very human Spanish friar, standing out clearly against the background of the sixteenth century.

It shows us, first, the little son of a poor widow, newly settled in the busy Castilian city of Medina del Campo. A well-to-do gentleman, struck by his ability and devout-ness, takes him into one of the hospitals to serve the poor in the intervals of attending the school of the Society of Jesus. But hardly is the boy of age than he sets aside his patron's further ambitions for him, and, in 1563, takes the Carmelite habit at Medina. Thence he is sent, for a three-years' Arts course, to the neighbouring University of Salamanca, which at that time numbered nearly eight thousand students and was of world-wide renown.

At the beginning of his third Long Vacation, there comes to the young man, just admitted to priest's orders, the decisive event of his career. Anxious for a life of greater austerity than that of the mitigated rule of the Carmelites, he has been considering a transference to the Carthusians. By chance, it would seem, he meets the great Carmelite reformer, St Teresa, who, a woman of fifty-two, has recently come out from a life of quiet recollection at Ávila to lead a campaign for the foundation of religious houses following the stricter and Primitive Rule of her Order. She has heard "great things" of this "young father" of twenty-five,[1] and sees in him the very man to stand with her in the forefront of the Reform—perhaps to succeed her as its champion. Will he join a reformed house for men so soon as she can found one? His reply, as she reports it, is significant. "He gave me

[1] St Teresa, *Foundations*, Chap. III.

17   2-2

his word to do so, *provided it were not long delayed*."[1]

So, after a final year's theology at Salamanca, we meet the young friar in Duruelo—a lonely oasis in the vast Castilian desert, where a peasant's hovel has been set apart as a monastery. Here he certainly realizes his desire for greater asceticism. As a Discalced Carmelite, he goes barefoot in all weathers. His cell is so low that he can only sit or lie in it; for sole adornment it has death's heads and roughly carved crosses ("¡Tantas cruces," exclaimed St Teresa, on visiting it, "tantas calaveras!"[2]). He sleeps on the ground, with a stone for his pillow. From Matins to Prime he remains at prayer; and in winter, as he prays, the snow will enter and cover his habit.[3] Such simplicity and austerity of life are leading him towards his desired haven. "The soul that would possess God wholly", he wrote, "must be possessed by Him alone. *Andar a solas con Dios.*"[4]

[1] St Teresa, *Foundations*, Chap. III.   [2] *Ibid.* Chap. XIV.
[3] *Ibid.*   [4] *Maxims* ("Puntos de Amor", Nos. 49, 57).

Nearly ten years of the friar's life have passed ere we again have a clear and detailed picture of him. The Reform has prospered; and St Teresa and St John of the Cross have made many foundations. But the main body of Carmelites has become more and more hostile to the innovators; there is open war, indeed, in the Order. St John of the Cross is for over eight months a prisoner of the Calced in a dark cell in Toledo; "hardly large enough to hold him," wrote St Teresa, "small as he is".[1] Unventilated, save for a hole communicating with the passage; unlit by day or night, save with a candle. There, on the one hand, refused so much as a change of clothing, the friar is starved continuously and scourged daily, and, on the other, is promised offices and honours, if he will renounce the Reform and return to the lighter rule. It is in the midst of such tribulation that he composes some of the earliest of his verses, notably the first stanzas of

[1] St Teresa, *Letters* (ed. P. Silverio), 246.

the "Spiritual Canticle", with their cry of
desolation:

Whither hast vanishèd,
Belovèd, and hast left me full of woe?

At last there comes deliverance, and, for the
next ten years, the documentary pictures are
set alternately in light and in shadow. Sent
first (1578) to Andalusia, the garden of Spain,
St John of the Cross forms some close spiritual
friendships by acting as confessor to the nuns
at Beas de Segura, a convent set in a well-
watered plain fringed by the mountains and
planted with poplars, pines and olives. Not
far away is the monastery of El Calvario,
where for eight months he acts as Prior and
enjoys the "still music" of solitude and of
Nature. The most productive period of the
Saint's life, from the literary standpoint (1582–
8), is spent at the Convento de los Mártires in
Granada—a monastery beneath a sky almost
perpetually blue, amid luxuriant foliage and
running streams; a monastery, above all, over-
shadowed by the eternal snows of the Sierra
Nevada. Here, as at Beas and El Calvario,
St John of the Cross finds peace of mind and

soul, together with such peace of body as is countenanced by his body's sternest master—himself.

But soon come storms once more. Liberated from the irksome control of their unreforming brethren, the Discalced Carmelites grow and develop freely, and before long find themselves suffering the pains inseparable from development. For a time, though by no means at one with the Provincial of his Order, St John of the Cross is a member of its inner council, is sent north again from Andalusia to his native Castile, and rules the central house of the Reform at Segovia. Then his fortune changes. His own brethren strip him of his offices and leave him to go out into the desert (1591). We see him at La Peñuela, in the solitudes of the Sierra Nevada, aged barely forty-nine but broken in health, and, at the end of three months, attacked by a mortal fever. Reluctantly, he leaves the place of his heaven-sent and welcome exile,[1] travelling, in search of medical aid, to the neighbouring

[1] "En esta santa soledad", he writes from La Peñuela, "me hallo muy bien" (Letter of September 21, 1591).

town of Úbeda. What he chiefly finds there is, on the one hand, the redoubled enmity of the proud, and, on the other, the friendship and affection of the humble. None of our pictures of his life are sharper and clearer than those which eye-witnesses have drawn for us of his death-bed, where the revengeful Prior (till the meekness of the Saint breaks down all his defences) enters his cell only to upbraid him, while monks and lay brothers vie in offering him comforts and seeking his presence.

Amid these moving scenes his life drew gently to its close.

Never weather-beaten sail more willing bent to shore.

He died at midnight on December 14, 1591.

These are the briefest and sharpest outlines of a life which, both in outline and in detail, must unfailingly appeal to the imagination. Most readily do we retain the image of the eager young monk accepting St Teresa's commission, of the prisoner in the dungeon of Toledo, of the beloved spiritual father of the nuns of Beas and of the unresisting victim of the disagreements of a growing society. These scenes become clearer still as we reconstitute the central figure. What kind of man was St John of the Cross? That "massively virile contemplative" (the phrase is von Hügel's[1]) was in this life hardly more than five feet in height and conveyed a distinct suggestion of the grace of femininity.[2] St Teresa, commenting playfully on his shortness of stature and at the same time on his learning, used to call him her "Senequita"—her little Seneca. Small features, a high forehead, deep-set black eyes and finely arched eyebrows bore witness to his gentle ancestry; his grave, reflective expression marked him as a contemplative by nature, while his quiet personality, says an early biographer, impressed itself immediately upon all who saw him. As we study contem-

[1] *The Mystical Element in Religion* (London, 1923), Vol. I, p. xxix.
[2] "Pequeñito y gracioso en el cuerpo; excelso y gigante en el espíritu; un genio encerrado en frágil envoltura." (P. Crisógono de J. S., *San Juan de la Cruz*, Madrid, 1929, Vol. II, p. 371.)

porary portraits, in pen and in pencil, we feel that here is an extraordinarily individual human being who can easily become very real to us, despite the intervening space of three and a half centuries.

And very real St John of the Cross has indeed become, both to those who have written of him and to those who have read of his life or in his writings. It is not those compelling episodes in his biography, one or another of which has served to draw many to him for the first time, that have exercised a permanent influence upon them. The roots of this attraction lie deeper. As we read of the Saint's austerities, persecutions and sufferings, there is revealed to us the purpose for which he endured them; and, as in turn we reflect upon that purpose, there is unveiled his innermost personality. Those who can penetrate deeply enough into that personality may find that they are already within St Teresa's "mansions", "in the seventh and innermost (of which) is the King of Glory surrounded by the most dazzling splendour which lighted

and adorned those mansions even to the en-
closure of the castle".[1] Those who cannot
enter so far can at least, and do, see something
of the reflected glory, which constitutes the
abiding attraction of St John of the Cross's
life and character.

II

The widest appeal made by St John of the
Cross is probably attributable to his poetry.
In his own country, and among Hispanists
abroad, he is famous as one of the greatest
poets of Spanish literary history: his three finest
poems have never been surpassed in Spain.
Unfortunately his output in verse was small,
and a great part of the little that he has left
consists of octosyllabic expositions of religious
doctrine, devoid of poetic feeling. Of the
remaining poems, several, while far from perfect, have a definite interest and a certain
beauty which deserve recognition.

[1] *S.S.M.* Vol. i, p. 163.

Among these are such paradoxical composi-
tions as the verses with the refrains

> I enter'd in—I knew not where—
> And, there remaining, knew no more,
> Transcending far all human lore

and

> I live, yet no true life I know,
> And, living thus expectantly,
> I die because I do not die.

The lines written in that dark prison of
Toledo, beginning

> *How well I know the fount that freely flows*
> *Although 'tis night.*

> The eternal fount its source has never show'd
> But well I know wherein is its abode,
>   Although 'tis night.

> Yea, in a life so sad and dark as this,
> By faith I know the waterspring of bliss,
>   Although 'tis night.[1]

And a little pastoral allegory, somewhat rude
in construction, yet beautiful in the simplicity

[1] This entire poem will be found, together with the three
referred to on p. 28, in *Songs of the Lover and the Beloved*
(London, 1931), from which the quotations in the text are
made.

both of its form and of its application, and attractive for the very daring with which the platitudinous love-theme is seized upon for sublime uses. The love-inspired shepherd-boy is Christ and we may suppose that his love is the human soul and the villain that comes between the two is Satan. The natural plaintiveness of the theme is intensified by the recurrence of a single rhyme and the repetition of the conventional refrain. I quote the last two stanzas:

"Woe!" cries the shepherd-boy, "Woe be in
   store
For him that's come betwixt my love and me,
So that she wishes not to know or see
This breast that love has stricken very sore!"

Then climbs he slowly, when much time is o'er,
Into a tree, with fair arms wide outspread,
And, clinging to that tree, forthwith is dead,
For lo! his breast was stricken very sore.

But the poems on which depends the purely literary fame of St John of the Cross are three, and three only—noteworthy also because they form the bases of four prose commentaries which are in reality treatises on the life of contemplation.[1] The poem entitled briefly "The Dark Night" inspires both the treatise of *The Dark Night* and also *The Ascent of Mount Carmel*. The "Songs between the Soul and the Spouse" are often known, like the treatise which interprets them, as the "Spiritual Canticle". On the "Living Flame of Love" the poet also wrote a commentary with the same title—in a fortnight, according to P. Juan Evangelista, his close companion, and (in his own words) "with a certain unwillingness... since they relate to things so interior and spiritual that words commonly fail to describe them".[2]

These three great poems force us, I think, even if against our will, to regard their author as "a conscious and skilful artist".[3] Those who dislike the attribution of conscious art to so entirely spiritual a writer must, first of all,

---

[1] Where the commentary is referred to, the title is given in italics; otherwise the reference is to the poem.

[2] *Living Flame*, Prologue.

[3] *S.S.M.* Vol. I, p. 269.

28

explain away the author's note to the "Living Flame"—a note found in every manuscript but one, and certainly genuine.[1] In this he briefly discusses the metre of the poem, which is an adaptation of the then fashionable *lira* used by the Italianate poets Boscán and Garcilaso de la Vega and by St John of the Cross himself in two of his other poems. There are reminiscences, too, in these poems of contemporary secular poetry, the importance of which may be minimized by those who wish, but cannot be entirely denied.[2] Finally, it is inconceivable that, however keenly attuned was his ear to the music of the sounds of his own language, St John of the Cross could have attained such wonderful effects of melody, such perfect rhymes and such exquisite phrases —so hard to forget, so impossible to translate —without conscious effort and attention to poetic form.

It would be doing the Spanish language less

[1] Cf. *Obras*, ed. P. Silverio, Vol. IV, pp. 6–7; Baruzi, *op. cit.* pp. 113 ff.; *S.S.M.* Vol. I, p. 269, n.

[2] See Appendix, I.

than justice not to repeat a few of those lines, the sheer melody of which has inspired men to learn that language, that they may possess for themselves an instrument at once so forceful and so tender, with cadences so delicately feminine yet with consonants and combinations of such roundly masculine sonority. The narrative of the pilgrim soul who sets out to seek her Beloved is told in lines of most ethereal grace. The rhymes are feminine in their entirety, nor is there a single harsh group of sounds in the entire poem:

Upon a darksome night,
Kindling with love in flame of yearning keen
—O moment of delight!—
I went, by all unseen,
New-hush'd to rest the house where I had been.

Safe sped I through that night,
By the secret stair, disguisèd and unseen
—O moment of delight!—
Wrapt in that night serene,
New-hush'd to rest the house where I had been.

En una noche obscura
Con ansias en amores inflamada,
¡ Oh dichosa ventura !

Salí sin ser notada,
Estando ya mi casa sosegada.

A escuras, y segura,
Por la secreta escala disfrazada,
¡ Oh dichosa ventura !
A escuras y en celada,
Estando ya mi casa sosegada.

Continually, in these poems, occur phrases which haunt us no less by the melody of their sound than by the beauty of their imagery. It is surely not fanciful to catch a suggestion of the divine transformation in the languishing cadences of the lines

Amada en el Amado transformada.

and

Entre las azucenas olvidado.[1]

The broad, dark vowels and the liquid consonants of "la soledad sonora" of themselves suggest "calm that can echoes move"; "profundas cavernas" penetrate far below "deep caverns"; and the "resplandores" of the

[1] The corresponding lines in the English version are:
Lover transform'd in lov'd, love's journey done !
Amid the lilies drowning all my care.

"lámparas de fuego" throw a light that is mellow rather than brilliant:

¡ Oh lámparas de fuego
En cuyos resplandores
Las profundas cavernas del sentido,
Que estaba obscuro y ciego,
Con extraños primores
Calor y luz dan junto a su querido!

And O, ye lamps of fire,
In whose resplendent light
The deepest caverns where the senses meet,
Erst steep'd in darkness dire,
Blaze with new glories bright
And to the lov'd one give both light and heat!

With all the love which St Teresa had for "Sister Water"[1] did this her disciple embrace the "bello e giocondo e robustoso e forte" "Brother Fire".

This last stanza suggests a second characteristic of St John of the Cross's verse—its preoccupation with the theme of darkness and light. Both in poetry and prose, his favourite image is the Dark Night, which also symbolizes one of the distinctive features of his spiritual

[1] *S.S.M.* Vol. I, pp. 152 ff.

teaching. It is applicable to two stages of the mystical journey: the one, from the life of the world, through the Dark Night of Sense, to the goal of Illumination, and the other from that illuminative state known as the Prayer of Union (the Fifth Mansions of St Teresa) through the Dark Night of the Spirit, to the Life of Union or Spiritual Marriage. Further, the Saint continually presents faith under the symbol of the Dark Night; plays on the symbolism of twilight, the black darkness of midnight and "night when it is near to sunrise" or "the peaceful night at the approach of dawn";[1] and frequently, with evident enjoyment, elaborates the paradoxical use made by earlier writers on contemplation of such terms as "luminous darkness", the "ray of darkness" and the supernatural light which is so blinding as to be to the soul thick darkness.[2] That for his prose. In his poems he gives his love of this theme equally free play. The "Living Flame of Love" is a paean to light, as is the "Dark

[1] S.S.M. Vol. I, p. 255.
[2] Ibid. Vol. I, pp. 254–6.

Night" to a darkness which is more truly light. For, as the pilgrim soul journeys to her Beloved, she is lit by "no earthly rays", but by the blazing splendour of "heart's inmost fire", whose properties the poet subtly transfers to the night itself with a boldness which he never shrinks to display, either in prose or in verse:

O happy night and blest!
Secretly speeding, screen'd from mortal gaze,
Unseeing, on I prest
Lit by no earthly rays,
Nay, only by heart's inmost fire ablaze.
'Twas that light guided me,
More surely than the noonday's brightest glare,
To the place where none would be
Save one that waited there—
Well knew I whom or ere I forth did fare.
O night that led'st me thus!
O night more winsome than the rising sun!
O night that madest us,
Lover and lov'd, as one,
Lover transform'd in lov'd, love's journey done!

A third attractive characteristic of the poetry of St John of the Cross is its debt to Nature— a source of inspiration which, until comparatively modern times, has been strangely to seek in the literature of a country dowered by Nature with such immense prodigality. It is of course chiefly by the "Spiritual Canticle" that St John of the Cross will live as a poet of Nature, nor can he entirely keep this theme out of his commentary upon it. The poem itself, from its first stanza almost to its last, is a canticle of Nature, a song of the open air, beginning with the Bride's cry of desolation as she finds that her Beloved has left her, passing to her determination to seek him and then describing the incidents of her journey which culminates in their union. Next the Spouse takes up the song. The Bride has enquired for her Beloved of "forest, thicket, dene", only to learn that he has passed through them, scattering a thousand gifts

As through these woods and groves he pass'd apace,
Turning, as on he sped,
And clothing every place
With loveliest reflection of his face.[1]

[1] Cf. here the *Silex Scintillans* ("The Search") of Henry Vaughan, whose poems so frequently (e.g. *S.S.M.* Vol. 1,

Now it is the Beloved's turn to apostrophize those "creatures" who had spoken to the Bride of his graces as she passed them by. All such he bids keep silence, that the Bride may slumber.

Birds as ye take your wing,
Lion and hart and skipping fallow-deer,
River-bank, valley, spring,
Heats, breezes, mountains sheer,
Things that chase sleep and fill the nights with fear.

By means of one Nature-image after another, the poet seeks to describe the Bride's new happiness. Now she rests in the shade of "the long'd-for garden, fair to sight". Now "blooms" the nuptial bed. Now Lover and Beloved roam the meadows, dally by the rivulets, penetrate the dark forest and mount

pp. 307, 308, 311) provide parallels with the Spanish mystics:

He heaven'd their walks and with his eyes
Made those wild shades a Paradise;
Thus was the desert sanctified
To be the refuge of his bride.

(*Works*, ed. Martin, London, 1914, pp. 406–7.)

to the "caverns of the rocky mine", to rejoice in a union crowned by Nature's glories:

> The gently moving air;
> The sweetest song of Philomel the queen;
> The forest wondrous fair
> On a night of nights serene;

(Darkness—and light!)

> The flame consuming-fierce yet painless-keen.

(Brother Fire!)

We ought not, here, perhaps, to shirk a question which has often been debated: how far is St John of the Cross indebted to the actual landscape of Spain—and especially that of Andalusia—for his Nature-imagery? For my own part I believe his debts to be very small.[1] Leaving aside the important question of his dependence in this respect on the *Song of Songs*, it may be admitted that he wrote at lovely Beas of "verdant banks" and of "purest waters...rippling o'er hill and glade", perhaps, too, of

> flowers and emeralds green
> Gather'd at coolest dawn. . . .

[1] Cf. p. 55, below and Appendix, II.

It may also be allowed that the commentary on this poem, the prose of which enshrines much glowing poetry, was entirely composed in the south and could scarcely be entirely uninfluenced by its author's environment. But we have it on the strongest testimony that images of no less beauty—those of the first thirty stanzas of the "Spiritual Canticle"—were evolved before their author had so much as set eyes on Andalusia, in the black depths of the prison-cell of Toledo. By the dim light of his candle, or in the brilliance of his luminous imagination, he saw distant hills, threaded by tiny streams, green meadow-lands spangled with gay flowers, the silvery depths of fair crystal springs. It was in his prison, too, that, after apostrophizing the woodlands beautified by the divine immanence, he sings of the nature and attributes of his Beloved in terms of daring metaphor:

My love is as the hills,
The lonely valleys clad with forest-trees,
The rushing, sounding rills,
Strange isles in distant seas,
Lover-like whisperings, murmurs of the breeze.

My love is hush-of-night,
Is dawn's first breathings in the heav'n above,
Still music veil'd from sight,
Calm that can echoes move,
The feast that brings new strength—the feast of
    love.

Those who (as I think) exaggerate the influence on St John of the Cross of his environment sometimes write as though it were disparaging the poet to consider his inspiration to have been independent of it. To me, on the other hand, it seems that no eulogy can be greater than the belief in his independence, for this assumes that, with the Scriptures and perhaps a few literary reminiscences as his only external sources, his unforgettable Nature-poem comes to us white-hot from his glowing imagination—and from his fervent spirit.

III

It is easy enough to understand that such exquisite and ardent verse should find an echo in the twentieth century, above all if its love passages may be given their most literal and sensuous interpretation. But how, it may be asked, can the asceticism of St John of the Cross have any meaning for us, in an age when the buffeting of the body, even in a figurative sense, is so distinctly out of favour? For years it has been the custom for writers on the Saint, outside Spain, to describe his austerities with at least a touch of disapproval. To R. A. Vaughan, in the mid-nineteenth century, he was "genuine" but "miserably mistaken"; his mysticism was "a dark negation", little more than "a fantastic gloom and a passionate severity".[1] "His own life", writes Dean Inge, in 1899, "was divided between terrible mortifications and strenuous labour." He "carried self-abnegation to a fanatical extreme, and presents the life of holiness in a grim and repellent aspect".[2] He "flourished", says William James, caustically, in 1902, "in the sixteenth century—or rather (he) existed, for

[1] *Hours with the Mystics* (1856), 9th edition (n.d.), Vol. II, pp. 152, 194.
[2] *Christian Mysticism* (5th edition, London, 1921), p. 223.

there was little that suggested flourishing about him".[1] Mrs Herman (1915) dwells principally upon his "inhuman detachment" and his "cruelty to his soul" which "exceeded even his indescribable bodily severities".[2] "Too often", writes P. Hoornaert more recently (1928), "we see in St John of the Cross the horrible ascetic, the man who has crucified his senses and appetites to such an extent that all their sensibility is lost to him, the man who has torn out his heart."[3]

That is, indeed, a common enough attitude, but I am not sure that either the teaching or the practice of St John of the Cross as regards asceticism needs any other defence than the recommendation to read his life in detail and to study his works as a whole. We are apt to lose all sense of proportion when our information is confined to salient facts and purple

[1] *Varieties of Religious Experience* (London, 1902), p. 304.
[2] *The Meaning and Value of Mysticism* (London, 1915), pp. 154, 176.
[3] *L'Ame ardente de St Jean de la Croix* (Bruges, 1928), pp. 19–20.

passages. The buffeting of the body, in the sixteenth century, was no metaphor, but was literally a common exercise of the devout. And, so far as records go, St John of the Cross was certainly less of an extremist in this respect than some of his Spanish contemporaries:[1] I think in particular of St Peter of Alcántara.[2] The primitive rule embraced by the Reformed Carmelites was indeed exacting and severe, but it was certainly neither "fanatical" nor "repellent". Whereas, too, both the return to this rule and the voluntary penances that individuals added to it, being the result of reaction against extreme laxity, might well have partaken of the exaggerated character of some

[1] It is right to add here that no records can be considered as conclusive, either on one side or on another, since on the one hand hagiographical sources in the sixteenth and seventeenth centuries are not always reliable, and, on the other, it was more usual to conceal one's penances than to publish them.

[2] The well-known testimony of St Teresa (*Life*, Chap. 27) to the mortifications of this Saint must be supplemented by the almost incredible narratives of his other and later biographers (cf. *S.S.M.* Vol. II, Bibliography, Nos. 1180–4, 1187–9, 1192–7, etc.).

reactions, the reader of the Carmelite annals will probably agree that they seldom did. There is very little in them to repel the reader of deep conviction and determined purpose, in whatever century he may live or in whatever country.

The teaching of St John of the Cross on asceticism, regarded from one aspect, emphasizes this point, for he very insistently warns his readers (who were primarily, of course, his own spiritual sons and daughters) against the possible exaggeration of physical penance. They must in no circumstances do penance at all without the explicit approval of their director; nor must they ever overtax their strength or perform any penance because it gives them satisfaction. Transgressors of these rules, he says, are doing "animal penance" (*penitencia de bestias*), neglecting the true penance, which is that of the reason, and gaining nothing by their purely mechanical actions.[1]

This surely is modern enough. It is when we leave the training of the body for that of

[1] *Dark Night*, Bk I, Chap. 6.

the intellect and will that the Saint's ascetic teaching presents some difficulty. Under both heads his principal theme is a renunciation, a detachment, a self-denial, an annihilation which are as complete as is well conceivable. He is one of the few religious writers in Spain who deliberately shut out created things from the life of the seeker after union. The first condition of his *Summa* of perfection is "to forget things created": *Olvido de lo creado*.[1] The golden rule for the journey to perfection is to "live in the world as though there were in it but God and thy soul".[2]

In the first book of the *Ascent of Mount Carmel* he sets out the principles on which he bases this negative part of his teaching. God is everything; all creation, by comparison, is nothing. "The affection and attachment which the soul has for creatures renders the soul like to those creatures; and, the greater is its affection, the closer is the equality and like-

[1] *Obras*, ed. P. Silverio, Vol. IV, p. 342 ("Suma de la Perfección").

[2] *Maxims* ("Puntos de Amor", No. 61).

ness between them." The soul, then, that would attain to "Everything"—namely, "union with the infinite Being of God"—must reject "Nothing"—namely, the creatures—for "that which is not can have no agreement with that which is". The force of this stark antithesis is strengthened by others: light has no commerce with darkness, neither has beauty with deformity, nor Supreme Good with direst evil. "All the beauty of the creatures," cries this ascetic, "compared with the infinite beauty of God, is the height of deformity." "The light of divine union cannot dwell in the soul if these affections [*sc.* for the creatures] do not first flee away from it."[1] So, in the Saint's own pictorial chart which illustrates the first edition of the *Ascent*, the "narrow path of perfection" is marked by the words "Nothing—nothing—nothing—nothing", while above we read

> Nothing dwells upon this Mount
> Save the glory and honour of God.

[1] *Ascent*, Bk I, Chap. 4.

Nor must the journeyer be merely "detached from that which is without". He must also be "dispossessed of that which is within" —"without attachment to the things of God".[1] To none of the so-called "means of grace" must he cling, to no spiritual consolation, to no pleasure (however pure) that he may find in devotion. "Come", cries the Bride in the "Spiritual Canticle",

> Come, grant me thy fruition full and free!
> And henceforth do thou send
> No messenger to me,
> For none but thou my comforter can be.

"Of all forms and manners of knowledge the soul must strip and void itself," says the *Ascent*, "... so that there may be left in it no kind of impression of knowledge, nor trace of aught soever, but rather the soul must remain barren and bare, as if these forms had never passed through it, and in total forgetfulness and suspension."[2] To the soul thus emptied there come the "touches of union" with God,

[1] *Maxims* ("Puntos de Amor", No. 46).
[2] *Ascent*, Bk III, Chap. 2, *passim*.

described in the "Living Flame", which prelude a more complete and lasting fulness. Therefore, we read,

In order to arrive at having pleasure in everything,
Desire to have pleasure in nothing.

In order to come to that which thou knowest not,
Thou must go by a way that thou knowest not.

For, in order to pass through the all to the All,
Thou hast to deny thyself wholly in all.[1]

Here, then, is St John of the Cross in his most unyielding aspect, pointing to that "lofty path of dark contemplation and aridity"[2] which leads straight upward to the Mount of Union—setting aside, on the one hand, physical comfort, the delights of Nature, the pleasures of art and all the "beauteous things" into which St Augustine plunged in his vain search for the Divine Beauty,[3] and, on the

---

[1] *Ascent*, Bk I, Chap. 13.
[2] *Ibid*. Prologue.
[3] *Confessions*, Bk x, § 27: "Et ecce intus eras et ego foris et ibi te quaerebam et in ista formosa, quae fecisti, deformis inruebam".

other, all means and aids to devotion, including (so far as may be possible) those supernatural visions and locutions to which the mystics are often charged with attributing overmuch importance. Can such counsels of perfection as St John of the Cross gives us here possibly make an appeal to the twentieth century? Unlikely as it may seem, I believe that they can.

First, it must be noted that such counsels are not given to all,[1] but to those rare souls who are undergoing a special training for the hardest of all journeys, the progress to divine union. Even the Night of Sense will be completely traversed only by the few; the Night of the Spirit is the lot of incomparably fewer. Those who are exhorted to possess "nothing" are after all on the way to gaining "everything". They are to embrace a heroic detachment only because they are bound upon a

[1] On this St John of the Cross insists so often that it seems impossible that those of his critics who write as if his rules were intended for all can have read him, except possibly in extracts. For a typical and perfectly clear statement, see *Ascent*, Prologue, § 9, or Bk III, Chap. 2, §§ 1, 2.

heroic adventure. We do not adversely criti-
cize methods of training, however rigorous,
which experience has shown to be effective in
physical athletics, nor look disapprovingly
upon the most appalling hardships suffered by
those who attempt to climb a mountain in the
Himalayas. None who believe that the summit of a mountain in the heavenly realms is
indescribably the better worth attaining will
begrudge those who set out to climb it either
their due and fit preparation or the perils of
the way. St John of the Cross and those for
whom he wrote were mystics, and a mystic is
a man who has fallen in love with God[1] and
seeks in this life to attain to Him. Let none
seek to separate the Lover from the Beloved,
nor to prescribe the means which she is to
adopt in her search for Him.

[1] This definition (*S.S.M.* Vol. I, p. xiii) having been
challenged by a recent writer, I take the opportunity of
pointing out that it is true both to the spirit of St John of the
Cross's poetry and to the letter of his prose, for he continually speaks of the mystic as "el alma enamorada". No
higher authority, surely, for such a definition can be found
among the mystics of any age or country.

This attitude to the heroic asceticism of St John of the Cross is, I think, at least a reasonable one. For reasonable persons, even if they doubt that the mystic's goal can be attained, will agree that, for those convinced of its supreme worth, the supreme effort is not too arduous. Further, they will welcome the existence in the world of principles clear-cut as a Castilian landscape on a winter's morning: they will rejoice that in every age there have lived persons prepared to risk all, and renounce all, because ahead of them they descry a horizon hidden from others, to reach which, be it but for "the flash of one trembling glance", they will cut down every obstacle that impedes them. Such souls, be they mistaken or only misunderstood, are the salt of the earth.

Thus much of the *askesis* recommended to advanced spiritual athletes. When he is writing for those of us who walk on lower levels, St John of the Cross has no scruple in making full use of the creatures. In the clear light of perfection they may appear to be deformity and darkness, but to the plodding pilgrim who hungers for refreshment they are, at the least, crumbs from the heavenly table.[1] Though not his chief—his supernatural—source of strength, they are "clothed with marvellous natural beauty" and thus "bear testimony . . . to the greatness and excellence of God".[2] In these last words St John of the Cross is quoting St Augustine and indeed he stands consistently here in the tradition of the Fathers. He desires (to quote one of his Spanish contemporaries, who sums up the patristic attitude) that we should "mount by the staircase of the created world to the contemplation of the beauty and wisdom of its Creator".[3]

So he counsels us, very explicitly and very humanly, as follows:

Whensoever a person hears music . . . and sees pleasant things, and is conscious of sweet perfumes, or tastes things that are delicious or feels soft touches . . . if he at once sets his knowledge and the affection of his will upon God . . . this is a

[1] *Ascent*, Bk I, Chap. 6.
[2] "Spiritual Canticle" (1st Redaction), Stanza v.
[3] Luis de Granada, *Introducción del Símbolo de la Fe*, Pt I, Chap. I.

sign that he is receiving benefit therefrom and that this thing of sense is a help to his spirit; and in this way he can use it, for then such things of sense subserve the end for which God created and gave them, which is that He should be better loved and known because of them.[1]

The only restriction placed upon such enjoyment and use is that we should not cling to it. And this not only because by doing so we sacrifice the greater good to the lesser, but because even from the lesser we cannot derive the fullest enjoyment "if we look upon it with attachment to it as to our own".[2]

In such a spirit of warm and living devotion, St John of the Cross unfolds all the treasures of his imagination and love of Nature in order to enhance the beauty of his theme. Contemporary testimonies, too numerous to be disregarded, bear witness to his affection for the creatures.[3] He would spend whole nights in

[1] *Ascent*, Bk III, Chap. 25.

[2] *Ibid*. Bk III, Chap. 20.

[3] The documentary evidence for the instances cited below may be conveniently read in P. Crisógono, *op. cit.* Vol. II, pp. 81, 82, 84, 86, 88.

prayer (we read) beneath the trees, or rise before dawn to walk for long hours in the garden until the heat of the sun drove him indoors. In his "heaven'd walks" about the countryside he would usually stop to choose a place for prayer, "near a spring surrounded by trees", while he would lead his fellow-monks to "some delightful stream or pleasing crag" and thence send them into the hills to pray. If it be objected that his search was only for solitude and not for beauty, and that he deprecates the choice for prayer of "a place that is pleasant and delectable to sense",[1] we may remind the critic of his quaintly stilted dictum that "God is wont to move the will to devotion" in places where there is "a pleasing effect of variety, whether it be obtained by the disposition of the ground or of trees, or by means of quiet solitude".[2] In the same spirit, far from condemning images, oratories, pilgrimages, ceremonies, and other accessories to

[1] *Ascent*, Bk III, Chap. 39. The whole chapter is inspired by an anxiety that more should be achieved in prayer than "recreation and pleasure and delight of sense".

[2] *Ibid*. Bk III, Chap. 42.

devotion, on the abuse of which he can write so sternly and so scathingly, he describes images as "most important for divine worship and most necessary to move the will to devotion. ... It is always well that we should employ them".[1] Did he not with his own hand draw a map of the road to perfection, giving a copy to each of the nuns of Beas for her breviary?[2] Did he not love, with his own hand, to carve figures of Our Saviour?[3] He is perfectly clear concerning the proper function of these things: they are "certainly lawful, and even expedient, for beginners" on the road to perfection. In progressing beyond a certain point, however, a man will of necessity strip himself of them. For St John of the Cross, as for our own Wordsworth, there is a

> still communion that transcends
> The imperfect offices of prayer and praise.

"Pure spirituality (he says) is ... bound ... only to interior recollection and mental con-

[1] *Ascent*, Bk III, Chap. 35. Cf. also Chap. 38, § 2.

[2] *Proceso apostólico*, Úbeda, 1628. Deposition of M. Ana de la Madre de Dios.

[3] St Teresa, *Foundations*, Chap. XIV.

verse with God. Though one profit, therefore, by (these intermediaries), this is only for
a time; the spirit will presently come to rest in
God, forgetting all things of sense."[1]

Once more, from a study of the man himself and of his writings, there emerges a
modern asceticism which makes a true appeal
to modern ideas of spirituality. It is quite un-
necessary to exaggerate (as some of the Saint's
present-day apologists have done) the signifi-
cance of the Nature-passages in his works,
of his artistic propensities, or of the literary
perfection of his writings.[2] We need not create
a new St John of the Cross for the twentieth
century: the ideals of the authentic Saint of the
sixteenth are still full of power.

Among the demands of the world to-day is
that it shall know things as they are. It shrinks
from understatements and euphemisms, rebels
against conspiracies of silence, refuses to live in
a complacency bred by ignorance of evil. And
St John of the Cross gives us things as they are.

[1] *Ascent*, Bk III, Chap. 39.
[2] See Appendix, II, and p. 37 above.

That devastating knowledge of human nature revealed in *The Dark Night* he gained by merciless self-examination and long experience as a director—not of saints but of sinners. None but is the wiser, the clearer-sighted, the more thoughtful for having read him. And, because the more thoughtful, the humbler; because the clearer-sighted, the more persevering; because the wiser, the more understanding, the more tolerant, the more compassionate. Knowing, he can understand, and understanding, extenuate and forgive.

This, again, is a pragmatic age, which demands that none shall preach unless he practise, and that the fruits of the preacher's instruction shall mature in his own character. And nowhere better than in the character of St John of the Cross shall we find the justification of his ascetic teaching. Of all the figures of the Counter-Reformation it would be hard to discover any at once more courageous and more resigned, more resolute yet more conciliatory, more outspoken yet more lovable. Rare fruits of the spirit ripen in the soil of detachment. The little schoolboy of Medina, the young friar of Duruelo, the persecuted reformer of Toledo, the poet-preacher of Los Mártires are but preliminary sketches for the all but perfected saint of Úbeda. Let us look at the letter which he wrote a few months before his death—broken in health, vanquished by his enemies, deprived of his offices, and banished to the desert.

As to my affairs, daughter, let them not trouble you, for they trouble not me. The most important thing is not to impute faults wrongly.... Think only that God orders it all. *And where there is no love, put love, and you will find love.*[1]

Surely here is the complete apologia for complete detachment—a degree of perfection attained, not by withdrawal from the world of his day, but by "suffering and battling with the actual facts of life" and by "recreating the world of men and things in the light, the blinding light, of his spiritual intensity".[2]

[1] Letter of July 6, 1591.
[2] Aubrey F. G. Bell. In *Bulletin of Spanish Studies*, Vol. VII, p. 21.

IV

We come, lastly, to consider St John of the Cross as what he chiefly was—a mystic. Properly speaking, of course, no such distinction exists between his ascetic and his mystical teaching as for convenience we are here making. The Dark Night of Sense is but a stage upon the road to Illumination, just as the Dark Night of the Spirit is a later stage upon that continuation of the same road which leads to Union. Too often the *Ascent* and *The Dark Night*, which are largely negative and mainly ascetic, have been considered as the Saint's characteristic works, while the "Spiritual Canticle" and *Living Flame*, which are no less characteristic, and deal chiefly with the illuminative and unitive lives, have been neglected. The result of this insistence on the negative aspect of his teaching at the expense of the positive—on the Night instead of on the Light—has been a distortion of his whole presentation of the Mystic Way and even a false interpretation of his character. A similarly mistaken insistence on the passive elements in his doctrine at the expense of the active led some of his would-be followers in the century after his death to isolate the passages in his works which speak of repose, and, forgetting to lay equal emphasis on those which speak of effort, to endeavour to father upon him the responsibility for the errors of Quietism.

As we rise, then, to the height of the Saint's great argument, to the glories of Spiritual Betrothal and the consummation of the Spiritual Marriage, we shall find, not a second picture, but a completion and a unification of the first. The task of those who would interpret it is not easy. St John of the Cross's mystical teaching is full of hard sayings. He moves on a plane so lofty that we cannot always follow him, even afar off. But if after much labour we succeed in overcoming the obstacles which cumber the lower slopes of his mountain, our effort will be richly rewarded. For the clarity of his vision, and the perspicuity with which he conveys to the reader what he sees, are hardly credible. The idea, commonly held and not infrequently expressed, that he is vague and obscure in his prose works is entirely mistaken.[1] He has the most exact idea of what he proposes to say, and all he says contains "a steadfast core of concreteness, a Castilian sobriety".[2] Applied to the sublime theme of Union with God upon earth, such concreteness and such clarity are nothing short of overwhelming.

He has the most exact idea (I repeat) of what he proposes to say: and therein he is like every true mystic. Have writers on mysticism perhaps spent too much time in trying to convince the world that the contemplative is as practical in the affairs of this life as is the active?[3] True, he frequently is, but by no means invariably; the children of this world are often wiser in their generation than these particular children of light. What matters primarily to them, and to us, is whether or no

[1] See Appendix, III.
[2] Aubrey F. G. Bell, *loc. cit.*
[3] Cf. *Spanish Mysticism* (London, 1924), p. 7 and n. 1.

they are practical in the accomplishment of that for which they have sacrificed everything. Almost without exception they are so; and St John of the Cross, one of the very greatest of them, is supremely so. It is because he is so practical, so clear, so definite that, for all its sublimity, his teaching meets with a ready response from souls like-minded but not always like-gifted in the world to-day.

The startling clearness and surprising full-ness with which St John of the Cross describes the Mystic Way has been surpassed by very few Christian writers, if by any. Many have written in great detail of their own mystical experiences: of this aspect or that of the Mystic Life, or of this stage or that of the Mystic Way. But they have seldom even approached St John of the Cross in compre-hensiveness. Of writers since the Renaissance it is his compatriot St Teresa who rivals him most nearly. To judge between these two would be a difficult task; *la Santa* has qualities all her own, but I do not myself find in her the sustained power of her contemporary's marvellous descriptions of the higher stages of the ascent.

No part of the journey does he leave untouched and unillumined. The chapters in *The Dark Night* on its initial stages show a profound and practical knowledge of psychology. They lay bare unsuspected motives, sparing neither penitent nor confessor. The Dark Night of Sense is described with a realistic wealth of detail; the bold counsels to walk in it by faith and to study to be quiet have found critics, but form in reality the only logical complement of the author's own description. Comes the dawn of the life of illumination, treated at greatest length in the "Spiritual Canticle", under the name of the "Spiritual Betrothal", and the second Dark Night—that of the Spirit—"incomparably more awful" than the first, which, for the few that are able to endure it, leads from Illumination to Union. No writer has ever surpassed the vividness with which St John of the Cross portrays this second Night; his keen psychological insight, reinforced by his own experience, gives us a document of priceless worth. In close relation with this state must be considered the chapters in the *Ascent of Mount Carmel* on supernormal phenomena and those in the same book on passivity. Finally, in the "Spiritual Canticle" and the "Living Flame of Love", the Saint attempts to make explicit what a less courageous writer would have been content to leave in the shadows of poetic symbolism: he describes the Spiritual Marriage, the summit of Mount Carmel, the Fire of Union.

To know him at his best, one must study his commentary upon those second and fourth stanzas of the "Living Flame of Love".

O burn that searest never!
O wound of deep delight!
O gentle hand! O touch of love supernal
That quick'nest life for ever,
Putt'st all my woes to flight,
And, slaying, changest death to life eternal!

How tender is the love
Thou wak'nest in my breast
When thou, alone and secretly, art there!
Whispering of things above,
Most glorious and most blest,
How delicate the love thou mak'st me bear!

What value have the mystics to-day for those who cannot forsake action for contemplation, who can take but the first few steps of the ascent, yet who yearn for the keen and pure air of the heights—who regard the great contemplatives with sympathy and admiration, feeling themselves, if secretly and in all humility, to be potentially of their family?

There are many such in our world. In an age more materially prosperous, spiritual idealism might be drugged by worldly success and few might be found to assay spiritual adventure. To-day we are seldom so beclouded. Thousands, in one way or another, are steadfastly seeking the ideal of their own vision. Perhaps they follow strange paths, are more than usually a prey to mists and fogs, more often than not find themselves fleeing from the Dark Night or stranded on a desolate and trackless hillside. But they maintain their ideal and seek in all directions for leaders and counsellors—not so much for those who speak with the authority of others as for those who can light them by their own experience.

It is here above all that St John of the Cross is such a matchless counsellor. True, he refuses to trust entirely to experience, which "may fail and deceive", and, "in that which is most important and dark to the understanding", he clings to the Divine Scripture, "for, if we guide ourselves by this, we shall be unable to stray".[1] True, sources can be found for him, in the Fathers as well as in the Scriptures, and some writers have thought (mistakenly, as I believe) that he was wont also to delve in the Middle Ages.[2] But none will deny that his mysticism is, in its main lines, and in most of its details, experiential. He has followed the unproven paths, has battled with the fogs, has missed his path on those bare hillsides, but missed it only for a time.

> Say that I roam'd in vain,
> By bonds of true love bound,
> That I was lost and that I now am found.

Above all, he has attained at length to the summit of the mountain. From that height he

---

[1] *Ascent*, Prologue.   [2] See Appendix, IV.

can rejoice fearlessly in Nature's beauty. He can look down upon the mists of faintness, doubt, misgiving, fear, attachment—those same grey, damp and chilling mists through which he has struggled upward. And lo! he sees them transformed into a cloud-ocean, whiter than snow, so that no fuller on earth can white them. With these first experiences of Union alone—to say nothing of its ever-deepening fruition—he can hearten those who toil in the plain; he has in fact so heartened them through the centuries and will so hearten them, we may believe, for centuries to come.[1]

Such mystics as he—and their number is small—can do much, not only for the few who follow them far up the mountain, but for the many who do so only in desire. They have described their experiences with "that eternal

[1] Cf. the article "L'union transformante" ("Saint Jean de la Croix a-t-il écrit pour tout le monde?") in *La Vie Spirituelle*, May, 1927. It is illuminating to remember that the loftiest of all the Saint's treatises, the *Living Flame*, was written, not for a religious, but for a woman living in the world, Doña Ana Peñalosa, to whom it is dedicated.

unanimity"[1] which goes far toward convincing us of the reality of the supernatural world which they have explored and won for themselves—that world which to one Spaniard was so real that he spoke of it, in those days of the new-found Americas, as "God's Indies":

O conquest bringing riches infinite
The conquest of God's Indies—world so great
And world so far remov'd from mortal sight![2]

That conquest represents "the everlasting and triumphant mystical tradition, hardly altered by differences of clime or creed".[3] And the upholders of that tradition certify us, in words that ring both clear and true, of a world alive and waiting for us to penetrate it, "as far as in this life is possible", according to the degree of our ability and will. They call to us: "O ye

[1] William James, *Varieties of Religious Experience*, p. 419. Cf. Henri Bremond (*Prière et Poésie*, Paris, 1926, p. 144): "Pour ma part, leur seule histoire m'assure que, pris en bloc, ils ne peuvent être ni des simulateurs ni des visionnaires. . . . Ils traduisent à leur façon une même expérience".

[2] Juan de los Angeles (*Obras*, Madrid, 1917, Vol. II, p. 404). The lines are attributed by the author to "a Castilian poet" (p. 401).

[3] William James, *op. cit.* p. 419.

that love, if ye will have fire, come light your lanterns at my heart". Or, at the very least, they invite and inspire us to adjust our own life to new standards, with our eyes fixed on their goal.

The mystical approach to reality is only one approach, but so direct is it, and so sure, that its study cannot be neglected by any one for whom reality has a meaning. And of those who have approached it most nearly, none has written of it with such clarity, such eloquence and such conviction, as that little serge-clad Castilian friar with the frail body and the mighty heart—St John of the Cross.

APPENDIX

I. St John of the Cross as a man of letters.
(Cf. text, p. 29.)

The literary importance of the work of St John of the Cross is, I think, unduly minimized by a number of nineteenth-century writers, and, in particular, by Rousselot (*op. cit.* pp. 382–3). "La Renaissance", writes Rousselot, "ne l'a pas touché davantage au point de vue des lettres: il n'a aucun souci de la beauté littéraire; et, si elle eût été capable de l'émouvoir, il lui aurait reproché d'être un vêtement plus fait pour cacher que pour exprimer l'idéal . . . Jean de la Croix ne semble pas se douter qu'on puisse mettre son soin à étudier, à imiter les Grecs, les Latins, les Italiens, même les Hébreux, ni s'arrêter à la poésie pour la poésie elle-même: il parle en vers comme l'oiseau chante, comme le cœur prie."

On the other hand, it is exaggerated by M. Hoornaert (*L'Ame Ardente, etc.* pp. 29–31), who writes of the Saint's work as "imprégnée du maniérisme de l'*Arte Nuevo*", with which "il aimera jusqu'à la fin vêtir la nudité un peu froide de sa doctrine mystique"; by P. Crisógono (*San Juan de la Cruz*, ii, 17–30, 137, 220), who, besides attributing perhaps overmuch influence to Boscán and Garcilaso, supposes that the Saint "must frequently have read the Romanceros"; and by M. Baruzi (*op. cit.* pp. 108–10), who believes that he used Boscán's translation (1534) of Castiglione's *Cortegiano* and probably the *Dialoghi di Amore* of León Hebreo.

That St John of the Cross, consciously or unconsciously, echoes Boscán, Garcilaso and Sebastián de Córdoba I am convinced: the parallels alleged, though no one of them is individually conclusive, are in the sum total far too numerous to be disregarded. But the reminiscences might quite well be the result of impressions formed by reading these authors in boyhood and never lost, nor need we for any reason suppose more than this unless we so desire. To believe, with Baruzi, that the Saint "made a technical study of Garcilaso" would surely be highly untrue to his character if these words are to be taken in the fullest meaning of which they are capable. More loosely interpreted, on the other hand, they contain truth, and, as far as M. Baruzi's treatment of the Boscán-Garcilaso question goes (pp. 113–22), there is little to object to beyond an occasional phrase and the use of the poem "Si de mi baja suerte...", of which, however, he acknowledges the authorship is doubtful (p. 117).

II. St John of the Cross as a lover of nature.
(Cf. text, pp. 37, 55.)

I have great sympathy with Mr Montgomery
Carmichael's protest (*Dublin Review*, January,
1931, No. 376, pp. 27–44) against the attempts of
P. Crisógono and P. Silverio to portray St John of
the Cross as an ecstatic nature lover, a "visionary,
ambitious, restless, dissatisfied poet", a "man-of-
letters, an artist, a sculptor, a musician", and still
more with his strictures on an article in *The
Month* for July, 1929 ("The Self-Portrait of St
John of the Cross") which describes the Saint as
"revelling" in poetry and joining a "group" of
young Carmelite poets (cf. Note I of this Appendix). Such judgments, untrue to the Saint's
character, are supported by no firm evidence, and
P. Crisógono (of whose book, however, I have
a much better opinion than Mr Carmichael) has
in certain of his deductions passed beyond the
bounds of legitimate criticism.

But equally mistaken seems Mr Carmichael's
view (cf. p. 38, above) that the three greatest
poems of St John of the Cross represent the
results of a "heroic struggle" to "obliterate (his)
fine natural feelings" (p. 31), or that, without the
Song of Songs, "there would have been no nature
poetry in the *Spiritual Canticle*" (p. 32). A critic
who takes this extreme view that St John of the
Cross had been completely "freed from the
natural forms of knowledge which went along

71

with his many-sided nature" (p. 35) must explain
the very existence of such poems with their
wealth of Nature-imagery; the author's clear
interest in their metrical characteristics (p. 29,
above); the preoccupation of the united Bride
and her Spouse, in the "Spiritual Canticle", with
natural beauty; and a good many passages in the
commentaries, one or two of which are referred
to in the text above.

Is it not reasonable, on the one hand, to reject
the idea (which surely no serious student holds—
certainly my friend P. Crisógono does not) that
the poet was offering in his poem "any *mere*
tribute of homage (*italics mine*) to the beauties of
nature" (p. 32), and, on the other, to consider that
"by the mighty efforts of his own heroic soul and
the merciful dispositions of Almighty God" the
Saint had reached a summit of perfection from
which he could look upon the beauties of Nature
and delight in them and sing of them with complete freedom from even fleeting and temporary
attachment, seeing in them, above all else, the
immanent God?

III. The Alleged Obscurity of St John of the
Cross. (Cf. text, p. 60.)

The idea described in the text is expressed with
characteristic and disarming frankness by Fitzmaurice-Kelly (*Some Masters of Spanish Verse*,

Oxford, 1924, p. 91). "The prose commentary of St John of the Cross is incomprehensible to at least one layman whom I, for obvious personal reasons, would wish to regard as a person of average intelligence. And he is not alone. The prose of St John of the Cross is of extreme obscurity to the profane." This idea soon vanishes when one *studies* the prose works, taking the same moderate pains to master the elements of mystical theology, and its distinctive vocabulary, as one would take to master those of any other science before studying a classical treatise upon it.

Further, only certain portions of these commentaries are devoted to mystical theology; large parts of all but one of them treat of matters purely ascetic. The early chapters of *The Dark Night*, on the seven deadly sins; the concluding chapters of the *Ascent of Mount Carmel*, on aids to devotion; long passages from almost any part of the "Spiritual Canticle" are typical examples. These and other pages, not written (as Fitzmaurice-Kelly asserts) solely for "highly trained confessors" and "expert casuists", but for simple monks and nuns of Carmel, are devastatingly simple in their condemnation of the sins of us all and winsomely plain in the way in which they point to the ideals of most of us. All these parts of the treatises he that runs may read, if he that runs has any desire to do so. The truth, it is to be feared, is contained in a well-known epigram by Mr Chesterton. St John of the Cross, like Christianity, has not been tried and found wanting; he has too often been found difficult and not tried.

IV. The Non-Scriptural Sources of St John of the Cross. (Cf. text, p. 65.)

St Thomas, St Augustine and St Gregory seem to be the Saint's only clear non-Scriptural sources. Apart probably from the pseudo-Dionysius, I believe that there is no proof of his having used any other writers, and such external evidence as exists supports internal evidence here (*S.S.M.* Vol. 1, p. 286). P. Crisógono adds as probable influences St Bernard, Hugh of St Victor, the *Imitation of Christ* and a few others; and, "greater than any of these", those of Ruysbroeck, Tauler, Suso—in fact the whole "German mystical school of the fourteenth century". Of Ruysbroeck he finds (*op. cit.* Vol. 1, pp. 40–5) only three "reminiscences" in St John of the Cross, one of which, as he admits, is simply of a name. None of them seems at all convincing, and, if we may consider P. Crisógono's "detenido y comparativo estudio" (Vol. 1, p. 40) as the "étude méthodique" which M. Groult desiderated (*LesMystiques des Pays-Bas et la littérature espagnole du seizième siècle*, Louvain, 1927, p. 175) in 1927, we may surely agree that Ruysbroeck's influence on St John of the Cross is negligible or non-existent. In the Taulerian sermons P. Crisógono has found (*op. cit.* Vol. 1, pp. 46–7) some parallels to *The Dark Night* which would be conclusive but for the commonness of their occurrence in ascetic writers, together with some less striking similarities. St John of the Cross may have known the works attributed to Tauler, or their sources, but it is hardly criticism to form, upon such slender evidence, these judgments (Vol. 1, pp. 45–6, 51): "Es sin duda [Tauler] el autor que más profunda huella dejó en el espíritu y en las obras del gran Maestro carmelita"; and "La historia de la mística no conoce dos místicos más parecidos".

Apart from the question of the identification of sources, it will be agreed by all who have read the mystics of Spain that none of them, except St Teresa, quotes so little from authorities of any kind, and none gives a more vivid impression of originality.